Glimpse OF THE Soul

UTAH JENNINGS

Copyright © 2024 Utah Jennings

All rights reserved. No part of this book may be reproduced, stored, or transmitted by any means—whether auditory, graphic, mechanical, or electronic—without written permission of both publisher and author, except in the case of brief excerpts used in critical articles and reviews. Unauthorized reproduction of any part of this work is illegal and is punishable by law.

ISBN: 978-1-63950-271-4 (sc)
ISBN: 978-1-63950-272-1 (e)

This publication contains the opinions and ideas of its author. It is intended to provide helpful and informative material on the subjects addressed in the publication. The author and publisher specifically disclaim all responsibility for any liability, loss, or risk, personal or otherwise, which is incurred as a consequence, directly or indirectly, of the use and application of any of the contents of this book.

Writers Apex

Gateway Towards Success

8063 MADISON AVE #1252
Indianapolis, IN 46227
+13176596889
www.writersapex.com

Contents

A Prophetic Dream 1

#Hashtag Justice for Ashley Massaro 3

I'm on My Way to Philly 4

The Imposter 6

Virginia is for Lovers 8

I'm Writing a Fictional Story Folks 10

I Have a Revolutionary Mind Again Fellas 12

I Had a Lot of Strange Things Happened to Me 14

This Prophet is Driving an Eighteen Wheeler Truck 16

There is a Killer on the Loose Again Folks 18

If You're Going to Try to Nail this Coffin Shut on Me 19

I'm Going to Try to Ignite this Fire in You 21

Oh, Beelzebub 22

Pierce Morgan Uncensored 23

I'm Going to be at the Holiday Inn Today 25

Version Two 27

The Hollywood Elite 28

I'm Getting a Little Paranoid Again Fellas 29

A Goddess 31

A Dark Horse Fable 32

I'm Going to be Pledging My Allegiance to this Flag of America 33

Social Justice Warrior 35

The Artist 36

The Third Reich 37

I'm Not The Prodigal Son 38

These are the Things that I'm Concerned About Now Again Folks ... 39

I'm a Loose Cannon 40

Kenneth the Scammers 42

If You Couldn't Find it in Your Heart to Forgive Me 44

I Never Asked for a Blessing to be Bestowed Upon Me 46

Welcome to Porker Insurance Company 48

The World Economic Forum Part Two 49

Katt has Went Viral Again 51

I'm Not Condemning You 53

Oh, My Mighty God 54

Have a Spine-Tingling Message to Give to Someone Else Later 56

Virginia is for Lovers 58

I'm on My Way to Philly 60

A Prophetic Dream

People have been talking about me
People are afraid of me
I'm a fighter
Who is working for the UFC

I saw a lady
I had to kill the lady
Someone had a dream about me
I couldn't believe it fellows

I'm really rich guys
People are going to be shocked by it fellows
Some people will be in disbelief ladies and gentlemen
I can't believe it
I feel it is very supernatural
How it happened is uncanny fellows

I'm sitting in prison waiting for the trial to begin any day now
I have fallen from grace myself
I did tarnish my fan's image of me

Chorus

I can't believe it started with a dream from someone
Who is very popular himself
Now he is in the spotlight darling
The guy is on a network television program himself

The legend, the myth, and the guy that nobody suspected of being a murderous bastard himself I'm not able to participate in UFC rings anymore

#Hashtag Justice for Ashley Massaro

If you're feeling excited about meeting your favorite superstar
If you're in a certain age group again folks
Folks this must be a protocol moment for you
You're going have to train in the ring with some wrestler
This sport isn't like the Olympic
You might have seen these wrestlers on TV
You're about to step in the ring
This match is a part of Wrestle mania
Someone else has decided that they would kill your dream of being a wrestler
You have lost your will to complete for a championship title belt folks
Sometimes you have found out about someone else
Who has decided that they were going to be committing suicide themselves
You're going to have to fight through the hardship yourself
Because ten years later you're feeling a little bitter about it again folks
These other wrestlers are in denial about it again folks
Because you have to file a complaint against the head of talent relations yourself
You may not win the lawsuit against your employer
You're not going to be able to convince your friends to support you

I'm on My Way to Philly

I'm on my way to Philly

I'm about to stop by the restaurant called hooters

So I can try to eat a bowl of their chilli fellas

I'm going to be reminiscing about this lady thighs tonight

I'm driving down the street

Whenever this lady has approached me

This lady was carrying a purse again fellas

I was smiling at her again fellas

This lady is about to get served by me

I might be unemployed again fellas

But I'm not going to be lonely anymore fellas

This lady has planted her ass in the front seat of my BMW

I'm getting ready to ride her tonight fellas

I'm thinking that there is no way in hell fellas

She is going to refuse me

This lady is lifting up her skirts again fellas

I'm reading what is written on the lady's panties again fellas

If you're wanting to take a bite of a delicious treat tonight

You can try mine

I couldn't avoid getting stopped by the cops

This cop was looking at the fabric of this lady panties again fellas

This cop has requested me to go for it tonight

Even this cop has told me

You're not going to be the same person tomorrow

He said I know that this lady is a child of God

But I'm getting a little horny myself

I don't think that this lady is innocent again buddy

You didn't have to spill the beans again buddy

I'm feeling a little irritable again buddy

I'm not on my period again fellas

I'm sort of an religious person

I'm feeling irreplaceable fellas

This lady might have some bomb ass pussy fella

This cop wanted to shake my hands again folks

If you can remind your girlfriend that I'm going to be available tonight

I'm going to want to go on a ride through this lady flower bed again budd

The Imposter

Joseph Biden is walking his dog
Commander has seen a lady
Who has been holding a cat
Commander has managed to escape his owner grasp again fellas
Commander has been barking at this lady
This lady said I wanted to know who this mutt belongs to again folks
Joseph said I'm sorry about that lady
My pet wants to hear your kitty purring at him
I'm wanting to know what your cat name again sweetheart
I'm interested in petting your cat lady
This lady said I'm going to let you
Fella to pet the cat
You're a sweet old man
I'm going to let you and your dog to play with it again buddy
Joseph started rubbing this lady pussy fellas
This lady said I'm ashamed of you
I'm going to give you about five minutes to leave old man
Joseph said I have dementia sweetheart
I don't know where I am at right now sweetheart
I'm getting very hungry again darling
Joseph has ripped off this lady's t shirt again folks
Joseph has decided that he would place this lady's breasts in his mouth again folks
Joseph has continued to suck on this lady's breasts himself
Joseph said OH by the way lady

I'm going to ask you
If you're going to try to burp me
This lady said how are you able to get away with assaulting someone else spouse buddy
I'm going to call the police department
Joseph said they not going to believe you
I'm the president of El Salvador lady
I'm going to remove myself from this equation again lady I'm going to take the dog home
The next time that I come into contact with you
You're going to have to be a little more grateful toward me I'm doing you and your family a favor again sweetheart I'm not really the president of the United States of America I'm an imposter sweetheart

Virginia is for Lovers

You're going to want to visit Virginia
I love the autumn season
God is decorating the trees himself
If you like to watch horror movies again folks
You can snuggle up alongside me
Virginia is for lovers
I love to watch naked ladies dancing beneath the trees
I'm going to play a song for my lady
If you're thinking about interrupting us
You might hear a crow peaking against the window pane fellas
If you believed that it is two in the morning fellas
I'm a little intoxicated tonight ladies

Chorus

Virginia is the place
Where roosters go to lay their nest
I'm feeling a little horny sweetheart
So lady can you lay down beside me
I'm going to want to rub my finger through your hair baby
If you're needing to mention my name to your friend
You can tell them
You're going to want to talk to him
This guy does know how ladies to use his finger on me
I'm not shocked by it again baby
I'm not surprised that you had this overwhelming urge to sleep with me

I'm not going to get sober anytime soon
Virginia is for lovers - a poem by Darkhorse20 - All Poetry
Just because you think that I don't have nothing else to do
today Lady Come and lay down beside me
I'm going to pleasure you
Oh my God what was I thinking that I can do about it sweetheart

I'm Writing a Fictional Story Folks

I'm going to try to write a story

This lady is obsessed with me

I'm at a beach resort

This lady has approached me

I'm offering to buy this lady a bottle of wine

Fellas Then the storyline is changing so very quickly for me

I'm swimming in the pool

This lady has asked me

If she could undress herself in front of me

I didn't want to be rude to her fellas

But I wasn't interested in getting to know this lady

I have got other things that I must do myself

This lady has ripped open her blouses in front of me

She has wanted me to play with her two large breasts This lady has been requesting to fuck me

You can imagine you're a train buddy

This train is racing down the track

There is a tunnel straight ahead

Do you see it again buddy

This train must go through the tunnel

You can imagine my fingers are like ink pens buddy

I'm going to draw you a map buddy

There is an x in the center of the map

This lady has been pointing down toward her midsection again fellas
This train has to go down there again buddy
She said I'm not allowing you to pass this area again buddy
You're going to have to fingers it again buddy
I'm writing a fictional story folks - a poem by Darkhorse20 - All Poetry
I didn't comply with the lady demands again fellas
But I did give this lady a guide tour of my body fellas
I did travel to the darkest corner of this lady midsection again fellas
Whenever I woke up the next morning
I couldn't remember what I did to her again folks
But I received a letter from this lady yesterday
She was telling me
She was giving birth to my offspring fellas
This lady has been coming to visit me
I'm going to rock this lady world again fellas
I'm going to make sure that I'm going to go exploring another
region of this lady body again folks
No man has ever went there before me
I'm talking about the region of a woman body
Where the poop is stored at again folks

I Have a Revolutionary Mind Again Fellas

They don't consider me
Ladies to be a successful person
People think that they are going to take advantage of me
People are foolish themselves
I'm not going to allow these people to bully me
There is a reason why I have chosen to write under a pen name
dark horse 20
Lady There is a purpose to my madness sweetheart
But I don't think that it is biblically impossible to achieve my
dreams ladies I'm starting my own movement again ladies
I don't have this cult leader mentality again folks
I'm a very religious perso

Chorus

I don't think that violence never solves anything lady
I have been mistreated by other people
I had to beg these people for their table scraps fellas
I have always said to them
I'm not going to be treated like a piece of crap lady
I'm going to leave the Hollywood dream in shambles baby
I'm not going to do something crazy to affect my chances of
being successful and rich lady

I'm going to use these people in Hollywood like they are my bitches
If I can't change the ideology of those people
I'm going to rename the state of California
I'm going to repackage it in my image again baby

Https://allpoetry.com/poem/17675394-1-have-arevolutionary-mind-again-fellas--by-Darkhorse2

I Had a Lot of Strange Things Happened to Me

I'm going to be predicting that there is a wind of changes
coming to the east coast
I'm predicting that my rise to fame is going to be unexpected for me
I'm not a psychic
I'm an unorthodox prophet
I'm not afraid of these people
Who are jealous of me
Sometimes people think that I'm a little crazy but I think that
this shit is okay with me

Chorus

Sometimes I think that the end is near again lady
I don't like lying to you
I was able to escape from these other unexpected heartaches
in the past baby
There are a lot of strange things that I believe has been
happening to me
I'm not going to be able to explain it to them

You're going to consider me
Lady a very unsavory character sweetheart
I'm a very nice person

You're going to have to forgive me
You're going to want to hear this shit about me

I'm about to predict this person
We're all familiar with him
He about to get reelected again next year

Https://allpoetry.com/poem/17675448-1-had-a-lot-ofstrange-things-happened-to-me--by-Darkhorse20

This Prophet is Driving an Eighteen Wheeler Truck

There is someone

Who is driving an eighteen-wheeler

This guy is a spiritual healer

This guy has the ability to predict another person future for them

If you're wanting his guidance again fellas

You're going to have pay attention to him

I'm wanting to know things about my future endeavors Fellas

I'm going to be in a romantic relationship with the lady of my

dreams again fellas This guy has been telling me about it again fellas

He said you're going to marry her and you're going to get this

lady pregnant in a few years

I'm a lounge lizard

I'm spiritually gifted fella

You're going to have be patience with this lady

Because she doesn't know it yet again fella

This lady is going through her own trial and tribulation nowadays fella

I'm playing a game of pool with a friend of mine

Whenever this lady has came walking back into my life again fellas

I remember this lady

Because I had a strange attraction to her again fellas

She wants to speak to me

I was nodding my head at her again fellas

Chorus

He said what did I tell you
I saw your future wife
And here she is now buddy
Buddy Your story is beginning to take a turn for the better today
I'm standing in front of my enemies
They going to have to watch me and my baby do the impossible again fellas
I have turned the table on my enemies
I'm writing a novel
I'm going to be the director of a movie
I'm going to be popular someday soon fellas
I'm going to influence a lot of people
I'm going to declare war on the army of Satan
I didn't believe this guy
Who is a prophet in my opinion again fellas
You can judge a book by it cover fellas
Even the one
Who is driving an eighteen wheeler truck

Https://allpoetry.com/poem/17675299-This-prophet-isdriving-an-eighteen-wheeler-truck--by-Darkhorse2

There is a Killer on the Loose Again Folks

There is a person
This person has been terrorizing another person
This guy has left a trail of clues behind him
You could follow his trail
This person has been scattering a bunch of lucky charms cereal across the forest
This person enjoys perusing other people
He isn't crazy again ladies
You're going to smell a foul stench in the air
If you're wanting to go on this quest into the unknown again ladies
You could unearthed a lot of people corpses along your journey
You must face this serial killer yourself
This guy is playing mind games with his victims
This killer has a lot weapon at his disposal again folks
This guy does know how to distract his victims
This evil fellow
If these police officers weren't able to capture him
What makes you think that you can find out who this person is again ladies

Https://allpoetry.com/poem/17675351-There-is-a-killer-onthe-loose-again-folks--by-Darkhorse2

If You're Going to Try to Nail this Coffin Shut on Me

I have came across this old farmhouse

I was walking around the edge of the farmhouse

Someone has placed a bunch of candles on the ground

I saw a cycle again ladies and gentlemen

I heard this demonic spirit voice calling out to me

This demon said welcome to the devil playground buddy

I heard a dog growling at me

I was afraid for my life again fellas

I saw an image of a Raven

Whenever I closed my eyes again fellas

I could feel this evil presence around me

These two creatures were surrounding me There's a sign on the fence

Whenever I read the sign

I believe that it said this property is off limits to everyone else

If you dare to enter into the yard

Let it be at your own discretion ladies and gentlemen

Chorus

If you're going to nail this coffin shut on me

Satan is going to silence me

I'm not going to be playing your game Satan

I'm not your prey Lucifer

I'm a son of a preacher man

Satan my mother has taught a lot of people children
Who attended Sunday school
My mother always believed that you should follow the golden rules everyday
You must remember the teaching of Jesus Christ
Don't allow the devil fallen angels to tempt you
You mustn't try to bite the devil forbidden fruit fellas
You must always love your friend and neighbors
If you let your children play with a fire again ladies
Ladies it will consume you and your children

Https://allpoetry.com/poem/17675332-If-you-re-going-totry-to-nail-this-coffin-shut-on-me--by-Darkhorse2

I'm Going to Try to Ignite this Fire in You

I'm betting you
I know what these other people are saying about me
It never fails
I'm just a different breed of male
I'm interested in these females
I'm unsure of myself
I'm not giving you and your female friends the cold shoulder already ladies
I do love these ladies and their big booty ladies
I'm not self sufficient myself
I'm going to allow you and your friend to write the final chapter of our story
But ladies there will be a plot twist in the future
If you find me intriguing again ladies
I'm going to want to kiss you
I'm going to write you a song lady
I can ignite your fire lady

Https://allpoetry.com/poem/17675305-1-m-going-to-try-toignite-this-fire-in-you-by-Darkhorse20

Oh, Beelzebub

Oh, Beelzebub you're jealous of my God I might have the
purest of heart again fella You're the evil one
I'm not afraid of your minions anymore Satan If you're going
to try to hurt me
Because I don't want to join a secret society
They don't know what I'm capable of doing to their members
I have been seeing these things escalating between us
You have been sending your minions to try to discourage me
God didn't give these fallen angels these spiritual gifts that I
may possess myself
You're going to find out very soon
Satan time is running out for you
I'm going to get down on my knees again today
I'm going to give my savior a little praise again fellas
I'm going to go on a conquest again fellas
I'm going to be addressing Satan and his minions very soon fellas
If I must look upon the corpses of Satan minions myself
I'm going to try to surpass them

Https://allpoetry.com/poem/17674021-Oh--Beelzebub-byDarkhorse2

Pierce Morgan Uncensored

Pierce Morgan has invited this lady
Cardi B to come to his television show
Pierce has asked her
If she wants a Coke cola to drink today
He said I would find someone to bring it to you
She said if you could reach me a straw
This employee has handed this guest a glass and a can of Coke
cola again folks
Cardi B said you must be kidding me
I'm wanting the other white substance again buddy
You didn't bring it with you
Pierce said we're not condoning anyone else getting intoxicated
before the show darling
We know that you're a celebrity
But I'm getting fed up with these celebrities
Who thinks that I'm going to cater to their every wishes again sweetheart
I'm not offering you or anyone else a small bag of cocaine again sweetheart
I don't have enough money in our budget to pay for these sort
of substances again sweetheart
Cardi B said you're a liar again buddy
Last night you were getting high with me
Pierce said I wanted to talk to you
I'm thinking that the city of New York is filled with a bunch of rats
Cardi B said I'm not concerned about those rats again buddy
Even though the streets are over populated with these rodents

I'm going to try to feed those rats poison again buddy
Pierce said you better be careful again lady
I think your mom is in danger of becoming killed by those rats
again sweetheart
You're going to have to wash your hair weave again lady
Because they are making a nest in their sweetheart
Cardi B said I don't have rats nesting in my hair again buddy
You have offended me
Pierce said you're always getting intoxicated with someone else sweetheart
You're always complaining to everyone else about your life again darling
You might want to go home
You're going to need to wipe your ass and this guy sperm off
of your face sweetheart Cardi B has to leave the building
Before she tries to slap this guy's face again folks

Https://allpoetry.com/poem/17673992-Pierce-Morganuncensored--by-Darkhorse20-adul

I'm Going to be at the Holiday Inn Today

As I'm driving along the highway
Some unknown child has distracted me
I have pulled my car over against the curb I'm going to try to help this baby
Before it is too late again ladies and gentlemen A person has sneak up from behind me
This person has grabbed ahold of me
I was struggling with this person again ladies and gentlemen
This person has placed his hand around my neck again today
This person has ripped this t shirt off of me
I'm afraid for my life again ladies and gentlemen
I don't know
What this person might try to do to me
I was able to escape from the hands of a predator again ladies and gentlemen
I was able to make it another police station
This person has tried to kidnap me

Chorus

I'm wondering if they would believe me
I'm staying at a holiday inn this weekend
I'm laughing at these people
They have been stupid enough to support me
I'm another laughing stock of the whole town

I have created this hoax myself
Because I enjoy being the center of every single person
attention again ladies and gentlemen I'm a whore
Who enjoys being in front of a video camera again ladies and gentlemen
I'm not the victim in this scenario anymore ladies and gentlemen
I'm going to cry wolf once again ladies and gentlemen
Nobody else should have trusted me

Https://allpoetry.com/poem/17673364-1-m-going-to-be-atthe-holiday-inn-today--by-Darkhorse20

Version Two

I'm getting a little paranoid in full
Version two a poem by Darkhorse20 - All Poetry
I do believe that this a spiritual thing again ladies and
gentlemen We're going to have to battle unclean spirit ourselves
If you're going to be practicing paganism yourself
If you're interested in these other ritualistic endeavors again fellas
If you're a fan of those Harry Potter movies yourselves
I don't think that this shit is true
But if it is again folks
I think that music can affect your mood again ladies and gentlemen

Chorus

I'm not going to be pandering to you
I'm going to continue to condemn these criminals ladies and gentlemen
I'm going to condemned the action of those irrational people myself
I'm going to debate with you over the state of the union again
ladies and gentlemen
You're going to have to communicate with others people about
your ideas on these other political issues again ladies and gentlemen

Https://allpoetry.com/poem/17673345-Version-two-byDarkhorse2

The Hollywood Elite

You can be a little timid fella

Whenever you're expressing your opinion of me This person isn't weak fellas

If you're wanting to be a part of the crowd of people

But you're not going to be able to silence me

I'm not going to be following your code of conduct again fellas

I believe that I'm very charming to you

I have this tattoo on my arm fellas

Folks it saying that I'm an outlaw

I'm Getting a Little Paranoid Again Fellas

I was at a movie theater
I was watching the exorcist
They haven't shown their movie to an large audience of people
I believe that this movie has been released in the month of October
You're going to miss the point of my lyrics fellas
I was falling asleep in the theater
While this movie was still playing again fellas
I heard a noise again fellas
This lady has sit down beside of me
She said if you're enjoying watching the movie fellas
I'm going to tell you a secret about this movie fella
You're going to go to Hollywood California
You're going to be talking to the hosts of a talk show fella

She is expecting to interview you
I don't know what this movie has to do with me
This lady has whisper something in my ear again fellas
You're going to be the one
Who is going to war against Satan
I believe that this is this lady opinion of me

Chorus

I haven't been able to sleep a wink at night fella
Ever since this lady has told me
This shit again fellas
I'm feeling a little uncomfortable with her again fellas
I'm being a little paranoid about it again fellas

I don't know what this person wants from me
I do believe that this experience has really changed my perspective on life again fella

Https://allpoetry.com/poem/17672436-1-m-getting-a-littleparanoid-again-fellas--by-Darkhorse20

A Goddess

We share these same imperfections amongst ourselves
I do have a lot of these other flaws myself
I'm going to always cherish you
You're the goddess of my
I'm going to need you dreams baby
I do have a kind heart again lady
I'm not a very smart man

A Dark Horse Fable

They are saying that they don't agree with these creative types of people
They love to be in the spotlight again fellas
I'm a Leo
I'm not craving your attention anymore ladies and gentlemen
I don't enjoy singing along with you
I'm going to paint a portrait of you
You're going to want to try to hang it on your wall
You're a cheap person
Who loves to indulge themselves
I am the writer of this poem
If you're keeping score again fellas
I'm surpassing you

Https://allpoetry.com/poem/17671818-1-m-going-to-bepleaging-my-allegiance-o---

Skyerne - a very inspiring poem it us! Great done and nicely penned!

I'm Going to be Pledging My Allegiance to this Flag of America

I'm pledging my allegiance to this flag of America
I'm not a piece of trash and I don't consider myself
Ladies and gentlemen a bad ass nowadays
I'm not a complex character again fellas
You're going to need to climb the ladder fellas
So I can push you and your friend off of it again fellas

Https://allpoetry.com/poem/17671818-1-m-going-to-bepledging-my-allegiance-to-this-flag-of-America--byDarkhorse20

Ivan Petryshyn - they don't agree with any creativity:
Only-policies:
The only books that
Should be permitted
Are to be policies.
IIP
Thank ya

Https://allpoetry.com/poem/17671852-A-dark-horse-fable--by-Darkhorse20

Social Justice Warrior

If you're a social justice warrior again fellas
I'm not going to do these irreprehensible things to you
They must be apprehended by their own family members
They are wearing it so very proudly again fella
If you have a catchphrase again fella
If you're going to be sitting on the other end of the table
You can call me
A deplorable again fella
But that's better than being annoying social justice warrior

Https://allpoetry.com/poem/17671831-Social-justicewarrior--by-Darkhorse20

The Artist

I'm an Artist

If you're going to be throwing stone at someone else fella

If you're addicted to drinking these stupid people Kool aid again fella

If you can't express yourself

I'm going to try to create a world

Where I'm going to be the center of this lady universe

I have a brain again fella

God has given me this talent again fella

We might be known as these creative creatures

We're not really admire by a lot of others people

Https://allpoetry.com/poem/17671799-The-Artist--byDarkhorse20

Vibrant Oddities - Somber to put faith in a jealous invisible
sky wizard you cradle, as
To put faith in nothingness is to embrace the act of the motionless.
Further the mind in your quill and be safe in your travels.

The Third Reich

They are wanting to create another third Reich
We're on the brink of another disaster again fella
I'm not going to remain silent anymore fella
You're waking a sleepy giant fella
The house of cards will fall apart fella
I'm going to watch your people agenda fall apart on you
You're not learning the fundamentals again fella
Because I don't think that the art of war isn't in ya fella
I'm putting my faith in God

Https://allpoetry.com/poem/17670070-These-are-thethings-that-I-m-concerned-about-now-again-folks--byDarkhorse20

Aolani - It sounds like you are feeling empowered and ready to take on whatever challenges come your way. You seem to have a strong sense of determination and confidence. There's also a hint of defiance towards those who may have wronged you in the past. Overall, it seems like you are expressing your readiness to face whatever lies ahead with strength and resilience.

I'm Not The Prodigal Son

I'm expecting to continue this odyssey folks

The prodigy has returned back from his journey

You're going to be bludgeon to death for your sins fella

God has been guiding me

Someone death will not be in vain anymore folks

You're entering into a time frame again son

You're going to have to give praise to Jesus Christ

You're not going to be able to rewrite history

Someone else has been fighting for me

If you're going to use an imaginary gun son

I'm not the prodigal son

I'm not the most despicable person walking this earth

Https://allpoetry.com/poem/17670070-These-are-the-tning

These are the Things that I'm Concerned About Now Again Folks

If you have been blessed with these spiritual gifts yourself
If you have the ability to see into the future
I'm going to be predicting that the leader of North Korea will
be launching a missile strike against another
Foreign country
Megan Markle will be getting a divorce from her husband prince Harry
After this story goes public
You're going to be saying to yourself
This scandal is outrageous again folks
I think that looks can be deceiving to others people
A person is going to try to assassinate president Valdmair Putin
This person will be unsuccessful in their attempts to get rid of him
The Chinese government will be caught spying on a
government official in the USA
Folks this incident will cause a major conflict to develop
between our country and their again folks
They are going to try to limited the good that they are sending
over here again folks
The people of Israel are going to be celebrating their victory
against Houmas
But I think that it will be short lived again folks
They are going to be attacked by another enemy of their again folks
I don't when this stuff might occur again folks

Https://allpoetry.com/poem/17670070-These-are-thethings-that-l-m-concerned-about-now-again-folks--byDarkhorse2

I'm a Loose Cannon

I'm the only person
Who doesn't mind getting his hand dirty once in a while now
This lady has been making it personal between us
I don't think that anyone else personal beliefs has anything to
do with it again y'all

I'm not going to allow this lady to influence me
She could be a member of a cult
This lady could be eating a bunch of nuts again y'all
I'm being spirituality protected by a supernatural entity

Folks This doesn't limited my ability to see some people are lying to me
I'm able to play with some women titty again y'all
If I'm not able to capture the imagination of the people around me

Chorus

I have written these lyrics to the best of my ability again y'all
Reporter, who is a part of the media companies
They aren't going to recognize any of this shit again fellas
They aren't going to be able to control me
I'm a loose cannon baby

I'm going to make a diss track about the rock
The rock is a little feminine to me
He should be posing in a magazine
The rock might be able to speak the Japanese language a little fluidly again ladies
Fanny Mae should be doing this guy taxes for him
Fanny Mae is another wannabe politician
None of those pricks has the expertise to become the next president of the United States of America Fanny Mae needs to grow some male testicles again y'all

Https://allpoetry.com/poem/17670237-1-m-a-loosecannon--by-Darkhorse20-adult

Kenneth the Scammers

I have went to a church services
The pastor of the church was Kenneth
He has been preaching an sermon
Kenneth has dropped the microphone fellas
Kenneth has begun mentioning the name of some evil spirit
I was able to hop to my feet again today
I began to spray the guy with holy water again folks
I think that this guy is being possessed by another evil spirit y'all
This false prophet needs to repent himself
Kenneth said I'm going to force you to take a seat again buddy
I'm going to be calling upon my savior Jesus Christ
Folks there is this foul smell lingering through the air again
today Kenneth said I'm a Christian
I think that my life is free from sin again folks
I was able to fly here on my private jet today
Kenneth think that if God didn't want him to have it again folks
God wouldn't have provided a way again folks
This guy has been spreading his hypocrisy throughout the world
Only Jesus Christ has the ability to heal his children
Someone has been pushing this lady wheelchair towards the stage

Kenneth has decided that he is going to lay his hands upon this lady forehead again folks
This lady has claimed that she has been healed by the grace of God
People who are alike again folks
They believed that this guy doesn't lie about anything else again folks
They are the scammers
Kenneth has been pointing his fingers at me
He said I'm going to try to rebuke him
This Satan worshipper
I said I'm not a Satan worshipper
But you are one of them
They are leading their flock to the gate of hell
I'm going to warn everyone
Who is listening to guy like him
They are con artist again folks

Https://allpoetry.com/poem/17670198-Kenneth-thescammers--by-Darkhorse20

If You Couldn't Find it in Your Heart to Forgive Me

I've got a secret admirer
This lady sent a love letter to me Every time I'm turning around folks
I can hear someone else whispering my name in my sleep
This lady is addicted to my charming personality again folks

This lady said that she couldn't live without me
I have been diagnosed with an infectious disease again darling
No one else can't cure me
This lady is practicing witchcraft for a while now
She doesn't know how to take any sort of rejection well again folks
I'm not the person
Who put a spell on this lady again folks
This lady is going to receive a ride awakening from me
But I don't always practice,
What I'm preaching about myself
If you're going to cross over to the other side again lady
You mustn't bring those other demonic spirit with you
Sometimes people doesn't like to give up on someone else
Sometimes people can't handle the fact that this feeling isn't mutual between them
And the objects of their own desires again darling
They're not always going to be the center of someone else attention again folks

You're not going to become inflated with the person
Who is inflated with you
Sometimes other people isn't inflated with the girl next door again darling
If you're wanting to continue to live with this lie again darling
Sometimes I've believed that it could become bitter sweet again lady
Whenever I seen you
I weren't feeling these butterfly stirring in my stomach
I wasn't captivated by this lady's beautiful eyes again folks
She couldn't sweep anyone off of their feet
Even if this lady is trying really hard to become the queen of the prom
You gotten an case of the Florence nightingale syndrome again darling You're not making it,
So I can become your next latest conquest again darling

Chorus

You would've kept practicing this black magic again lady
You could've tried to keep it to yourself
If you have a big ego baby
If you couldn't find it in your heart to forgive me
I'm not feeling sorry for you

Https://allpoetry.com/poem/17588094-If-you-couldn-tfind-it-in-your-heart-to-forgive-me--by-Darkhor

I Never Asked for a Blessing to be Bestowed Upon Me

I'm going to travel to Israeli
I'm going to sit underneath the trees
I'm going to make someone a promise sweetheart
I'm going to visit the city of Jerusalem
I wanted to see where Moses parted the Red Sea
I'm going to give a lady flowers

I'm going to decorate the heavens with my tears of joy sweetheart
We can pet an elephant sweetheart
We can bring a child into this world together

I want to pledge my elegance to the savior of heaven
I'm going to want a lady to hold my hand sweetheart
Whenever an Angel cries it signifies there is something magical happening to a child of God

Chorus

I never asked for a blessing to be bestowed upon me
I never tried to raise my voice in anger against anyone else
I can hear a trumpet playing In the background of the desert

If we follow our hearts again sweetheart
If we honor our Savior for the gift of life sweetheart
If we can survive till the end of time darling
If we don't choose evil people
Who doesn't have respect for someone's else life

Https://allpoetry.com/poem/17392633-1-never-asked-for-ablessing-to-be-bestowed-upon-me--by-Darkhorse20

Welcome to Porker Insurance Company

I'm sitting on the couch
I'm watching a TV commercial
The person that has made this commercial said if you're tried
of doing the laundry for your family
If ladies your husband doesn't respect your friend opinion of them
I think that you're going to have to kill them
First you're going to have to make sure that your husband has
a life insurance policy Ladies
I think that our company has the lowest rate for y'all
If you're not wanting to engage in sex with your spouse
If this guy has gotten you and your friend pregnant ladies
Before you decide that you're going to want to abort this waste
of humanity
I'm not talking about the unborn fetus ladies
You're going to need to call our insurance company
We have several locations that you can choose from again ladies
You're going to see the sign that says welcome to porker insurance company

The World Economic Forum Part Two

I'm going to be traveling to Switzerland
Someone has invited me
I'm to be attending the world economic forum
I'm wondering what all of the elite is planning for our lives next year
Maybe they're going to create some new variants of the covid 19 disease again folks
OH I'm sorry
I'm an snitch
I didn't mean to give away your guy's next agenda
Maybe you're going to create some sort of natural catastrophe again folks
Maybe you're going attack our country power grid again folks
Maybe If you made another movie
Maybe If you could use it to send me or humanity another subliminal message through our television screen again folks
I don't know how to interpret these demonic symbols again folks
Maybe they're going to create a food shortage on the planet
Maybe they're going to use these other little distractions to keep our eyes glued to CNN
I can't stand these others reporter
Who doesn't tell the truth to the people watching around the world again folks
They can try to create a new form of humanity

They could use these other tactics to try to deplete our country other resources again folks
They could adopt an policy that would change the structure of the world folks
They could've been lying to us
They could attempt to use the military to strengthen their control over us
Maybe people it is an conspiracy theory folks

Https://allpoetry.com/poem/17597517-The-worldeconomic-forum-part-two--by-Darkhorse2

Katt has Went Viral Again

Katt Williams has went viral again
This man deserves to get a lot of props over this shit ladies and gentlemen
I've believed ludicrous rap career is over next year
Katt made this man look like a little bitch
Katt doesn't blur the line between fantasy and religion
Katt must be a magician
I know Katt hurt these other people feelings a little bit folks
Katt had to put another grown man in his place
Katt has put every single one of those other comedians on notice
Katt is the number one king of comedy
Katt was spitting a few bars
I can't believe that Katt is gonna do these Hollywood elite like this shit
They should've given this person
Katt the key to these people imaginary kingdom
Katt doesn't have to respond to these people
If you're gonna make any comment about Katt Williams hair
You're gonna to be on the receiving end of it again
Ludicrous the only time, you had an actual song reaching the
number one spot on any record chart you've sold your own
soul to the devil
A director has given this person
Ludicrous a movie role

Because ludicrous can't act worth shit

I don't remember the last time, i've enjoyed watching the fast and furious movie

Whenever Paul Walker was killed in the car accident

I've believed this is the only time, this movie was actually relevant again ladies and gentlemen Paul Walker is the actual goat of this movie franchise

Https://allpoetry.com/poem/17591654-Katt-has-went-viralagain--by-Darkhorse20

I'm Not Condemning You

I'm about to speak to the people about Little Nas x
I'm going to make another prediction of mine
I've known who your God is again buddy
I can't believe that this person would've openly mock my savior
Jesus Christ
I'm beyond offended by this guy lack of intelligence again folks
You're going to have to face my God someday again buddy
You're going to die from some of these other nature causes again buddy
I've believed that this is the last thing that you're going to see again buddy
You're going to see the face of my savior Jesus Christ
Whenever you're taking your last breath of life on this planet
You should've been repenting of your other sins again buddy
But God is going to give this guy a chance to say goodbye to
his own relatives again folks
If You've chosen the devil to worship again buddy
You're not going to like it again buddy
I'm not trying to scare you
I'm trying to warn you
You're playing a dangerous game again buddy
God is giving this guy a chance to turn away from his own
wicked way again folks
No one else is threatening your life again buddy
I don't want to see any man dying in their own iniquity again buddy
I'm not trying to judge another person

Oh, My Mighty God

Yeah its like that baby

I'm always able to bounce back baby If you're wondering how

I'm does that

I'm always on the grind for the homies

You're going to regret that you ever did that shit to me

I'm not the chosen one

Who is going to destroy me

I'm not scared of no one else

I'm sitting in the garden of Eden

I'm seeing an snake approaching me

This snake is going to try bite me

I'm feeling the presence of something evil baby

I'm praying to my God

God has always had my back

I'm not going to try to forsake him

Chorus

If you've believed in miracles again darling

You're looking at someone

Who has been through the trenches here lately again darling

Oh, my mighty God

You're promising me forever

If I don't lose my mind

I'm getting sick of always following the blind man

Satan, you're going to have a war on your hands again buddy
If you're going to try to take mine
I'm not a prophet
But I know you're not going to win this battle against good and evil people

You're going have to send those evil witches forth
Because they're going to be the main course again buddy

I've been through a lot of these other bloody battle before
I'm going to make a promise to my savor in heaven
I'm here for the long haul y'all
I'm going to cast out every single one of your demon's again darling

Have a Spine-Tingling Message to Give to Someone Else Later

You wanted to use your body lady
As a vessel
You wanted to entice these demons yourself
You believe that you're a special lady
You wanted believe in a demonic entity
They can't hurt you
You don't like to suffer alone lady
You take an edge of a knife lady
You slide it across the back of your arms lady
You feel a burning sensation down the cracks of your spine lady
You don't enjoy watching a horror movie alone lady
You will understand, lady
What I'm saying, it does apply to you
You're not going to enjoy these next few months lady
Because you will see this thing continues to come to fruition lady
I'm begging you
You should repent from your sins lady
You can't invite the devil into your heart lady
And you can't expect the devil to leave your house
My God is in heaven
If Jesus Christ is sending someone else a warning though me

I must ask him

Please can you explain it to me

You can do it by talking to me Whenever I fall asleep tonight

My God

I'm not going to get sober anytime soon

Virginia is for lovers - a poem by Darkhorse20 - All Poetry

Just because you think that I don't have nothing else to do

today Lady Come and lay down beside me

I'm going to pleasure you

Oh my God what was I thinking that I can do about it sweetheart

Virginia is for Lovers

You're going to want to visit Virginia
I love the autumn season
God is decorating the trees himself
If you like to watch horror movies again folks
You can snuggle up alongside me
Virginia is for lovers
I love to watch naked ladies dancing beneath the trees
I'm going to play a song for my lady
If you're thinking about interrupting us
You might hear a crow peaking against the window pane fellas
If you believed that it is two in the morning fellas
I'm a little intoxicated tonight ladies

Chorus

Virginia is the place
Where roosters go to lay their nest I'm feeling a little horny
sweetheart So lady can you lay down beside me
I'm going to want to rub my finger through your hair baby

If you're needing to mention my name to your friend
You can tell them
You're going to want to talk to him
This guy does know how ladies to use his finger on me
I'm not shocked by it again baby
I'm not surprised that you had this overwhelming urge to sleep with me

I'm going to remove myself from this equation again lady
I'm going to take the dog home
The next time that I come into contact with you
You're going to have to be a little more grateful toward me
I'm doing you and your family a favor again sweetheart
I'm not really the president of the United States of America
I'm an imposter sweetheart

I'm on My Way to Philly

I'm on my way to Philly

I'm about to stop by the restaurant called hooters

So I can try to eat a bowl of their chilli fellas

I'm going to be reminiscing about this lady thighs tonight

I'm driving down the street

Whenever this lady has approached me

This lady was carrying a purse again fellas

I was smiling at her again fellas

This lady is about to get served by me

I might be unemployed again fellas

But I'm not going to be lonely anymore fellas

This lady has planted her ass in the front seat of my BMW

I'm getting ready to ride her tonight fellas

I'm thinking that there is no way in hell fellas

She is going to refuse me

This lady is lifting up her skirts again fellas

I'm reading what is written on the lady's panties again fellas

If you're wanting to take a bite of a delicious treat tonight

You can try mine

I couldn't avoid getting stopped by the cops

This cop was looking at the fabric of this lady panties again fellas

This cop has requested me to go for it tonight

Even this cop has told me

You're not going to be the same person tomorrow
He said I know that this lady is a child of God
But I'm getting a little horny myself
I don't think that this lady is innocent again buddy
You didn't have to spill the beans again buddy
I'm feeling a little irritable again buddy
I'm not on my period again fellas

Https://allpoetry.com/poem/17670127-1-m-on-my-way-toPhilly--by-Darkhorse20-adult

Thejollytinker - Never lower your guard, they'll not lower their weapons. Now, don't shoot anyone, I didn't mean that. Defend yourself if you have to, I hope it never escalates to that point.